GARDENS
Maine Style
DAYBOOK

Down East Books

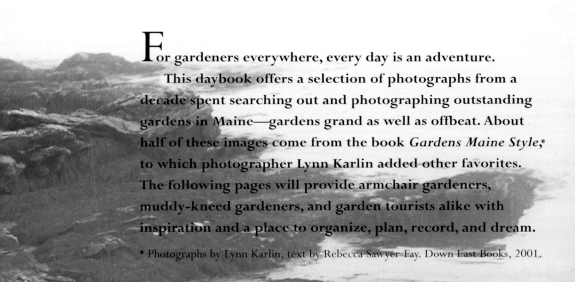

For gardeners everywhere, every day is an adventure.

This daybook offers a selection of photographs from a decade spent searching out and photographing outstanding gardens in Maine—gardens grand as well as offbeat. About half of these images come from the book *Gardens Maine Style,*• to which photographer Lynn Karlin added other favorites. The following pages will provide armchair gardeners, muddy-kneed gardeners, and garden tourists alike with inspiration and a place to organize, plan, record, and dream.

• Photographs by Lynn Karlin, text by Rebecca Sawyer-Fay. Down East Books, 2001.

January

January 1

January 4

January 2

January 5

January 3

January 6

Winterberries encased in ice.

January 7

January 10

January 8

January 11

January 9

January 12

A rustic gate adds winter interest and hints at what will follow . . .

January 13

January 16

January 14

January 17

January 15

January 18

January 19

January 22

January 20

January 23

January 21

January 24

January 25

January 28

January 26

January 29

January 27

January 30

Herbs abound where snow once clung.

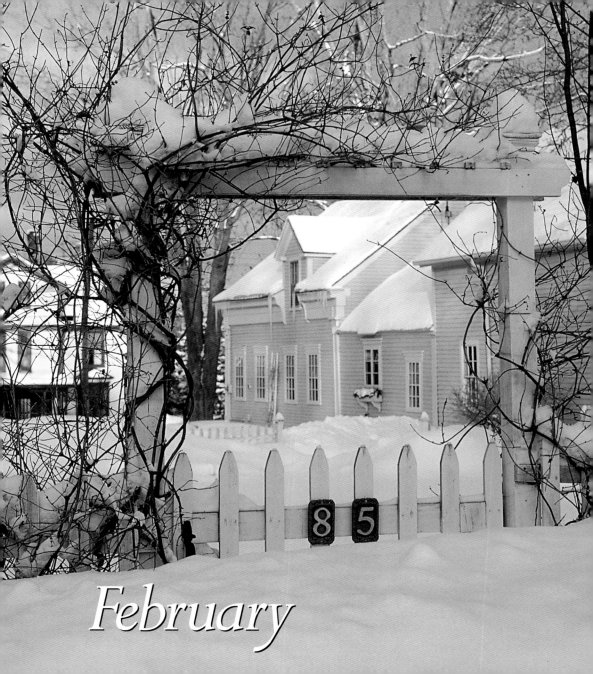

February

February 1

February 2

February 3

February 4

February 5

February 6

A homemade arbor frames a winter scene.

February 7

February 10

February 8

February 11

February 9

February 12

Ice storms leave a jewel-like setting.

February 13

February 14

February 15

February 16

February 17

February 18

February 19

February 20

February 21

February 22

Herbal Magic

February is a good time to think about what herbs to plant in your garden. Consider including both medicinal and culinary plants. Maine's Native Americans knew the value of indigenous plants and, later on, settlers "from away" brought other beneficial plants with them, some of which became naturalized in their new habitat. Today, with their popularity at an all-time high, herbs have become a veritable industry. Medicine cabinets are once again stocked with salves, tinctures, and soaps from companies offering Maine-made herbal preparations.

February 23

February 26

February 24

February 27

February 25

February 28/29

Alder branches in a ladder-back pattern make a handsome fence.

March

March 1

March 4

March 2

March 5

March 3

March 6

Ideas for garden fences and walls include:
'Carefree Beauty' and 'Bonica' roses cascading in romantic profusion over a picket fence . . .

March 7

March 8

March 9

Voluptuous hydrangeas spilling over
weathered rails . . .

March 10

March 13

March 11

March 14

March 12

March 15

Fenced-In

E lements that can turn a plain-Jane homesite into a charming camp-style garden include window boxes, paths, fences, and stone walls. Fences, especially, can offer handsome support for top-heavy plants such as rambling roses, flowering vines, or even climbing hydrangeas. Moreover, they can serve as a backdrop for mixed borders of annuals, perennials, and herbs. Split-rail, picket, alder or maple saplings, and bent-willow are all styles to consider.

March 20

March 23

March 21

March 24

March 22

March 25

Crenellated stones crowning a granite wall . . .

March 26

March 27

March 28

March 29

March 30

March 31

Potted pelargoniums in bright hues enlivening a formal white fence.

April

April 1

April 4

April 2

April 5

April 3

April 6

'Pickwick' crocus announce spring.

April 7

April 10

April 8

April 11

April 9

April 12

Rhubarb arrived in America in the 1790s, courtesy of a Maine farmer who imported stock from England.

April 13

April 16

April 14

April 17

April 15

April 18

April 19

April 22

April 20

April 23

April 21

April 24

April 25

April 28

April 26

April 29

April 27

April 30

An old display carousel shows vintage seed packets and advertising cards.

May

May 1

May 4

May 2

May 5

May 3

May 6

A terraced slope and stone wall provide a showcase for flowering bulbs.

May 7

May 10

May 8

May 11

May 9

May 12

The intoxicating scent of lilacs entices guests to the porch.

May 13

May 14

May 15

May 16

May 17

May 18

May 19

May 20

May 21

May 22

Grow an Antique

Despite Maine's frigid winters and fierce ice storms, some plants flourish for decades. Almost always, species with the greatest endurance survive because they require little or no care. The gardeners who first put them in the ground are seldom around as the plants enter old age. Living antiques such as lilacs, peonies, gas plants, and peewee hydrangeas are extremely tough, surviving Maine's most brutal winter storms.

M a y 23

M a y 26

M a y 24

M a y 27

M a y 25

M a y 28

The time-honored custom of dividing and sharing root stock ensures a peony's survival for generations to come.

May 29

May 30

May 31

Hardy kiwi vine cloaks a handmade rustic arbor.

June

June 1

June 4

June 2

June 5

June 3

June 6

The simple beauty of naturalized lupine symbolizes the approach of summer.

June 7

June 10

June 8

June 11

June 9

June 12

A Maine version of an Elizabethan parterre features flowering thyme, oyster shells, and mussel shells.

June 13

June 16

June 14

June 17

June 15

June 18

June 19

June 20

June 21

June 22

June 23

June 24

June 25

June 28

June 26

June 29

June 27

June 30

An array of roses softens a coastal garden shed.

July

July 1

July 4

July 2

July 5

July 3

July 6

Deadheading hybrid rugosas encourages rebloom.

July 7

July 10

July 8

July 11

July 9

July 12

A seaside cottage porch is "planted" with flowers that appeal to hummingbirds and other pollinators.

July 13

July 14

The Joy of Roses

I n a challenging climate, selecting
the right rose variety is the key
to success. Consider the Gallicas
and damasks, two classifications that
stand up well to tough winters.
Modern shrub roses, too, are worth
a try. Other good bets for coastal
gardens include the justly famous
rugosa roses. In return for no prun-
ing or staking, rugosas give decades
of joy. Today, what many people
think of as "wild beach roses" can be
cultivated in home gardens in a
wide variety of forms and colors.

July 15

July 16

July 17

July 20

July 18

July 21

July 19

July 22

July 23

July 24

July 25

July 26

July 27

July 28

The colors of 'Freisinger Morgenrote' can vary depending on growing conditions.

July 29

July 30

July 31

Container plantings add to the whimsical
"dooryard" of a vintage house trailer.

August

August 1

August 4

August 2

August 5

August 3

August 6

Mass plantings, such as this lavender, make a dramatic statement.

August 7

August 10

August 8

August 11

August 9

August 12

Colorful annuals jazz up gardens and tabletops alike.

August 13

August 16

August 14

August 17

August 15

August 18

August 19

August 20

August 21

August 22

An Annual Affair

Annuals that have filled vases
in Maine for generations
include bachelor's buttons, calen-
dula, China asters, zinnias, cosmos.
With regular deadheading, all these
annuals will bloom continuously
until hit by autumn frost. If short
on space, consider designing
containers to grow your favorite
varieties. Recycled washtubs,
old coffee cans, and even decom-
missioned rowboats are just a few
possibilities for displaying flowers
with style.

August 23

August 24

August 25

Even kittens love blueberries.

August 26

August 29

August 27

August 30

August 28

August 31

Hydrangeas (*H. macrophylla* 'Nikko Blue') echo the bright blue sea and the cottage's painted trim.

September

September 1

September 4

September 2

September 5

September 3

September 6

Nestled in a vintage lawn chair, gourds and bittersweet conspire in a vibrant still life.

September 7

September 10

September 8

September 11

September 9

September 12

A kitchen garden can be wonderfully colorful.

September 13

September 16

September 14

September 17

September 15

September 18

September 19

September 22

September 20

September 23

September 21

September 24

September 25

September 28

September 26

September 29

September 27

September 30

On a bed of blue dianthus, a fallen maple leaf signals summer's end.

October

October 1

October 2

October 3

October 4

October 5

October 6

On a warm autumn afternoon, a honeysuckle bower invites quiet contemplation.

October 7

October 10

October 8

October 11

October 9

October 12

A golden harvest of onions, braided for display and convenience.

October 13

October 14

October 15

October 16

October 17

October 18

October 19

October 20

October 21

October 22

Glorious Pumpkins and Gourds

W hile you *can* dine on squash and pumpkins, you can't on ornamental gourds (*Cucurbita pepo* var. *ovifern*). Edible or not, all members of the Cucurbitaceae family do catch the eye in a colorful display. Sun-loving gourds are easily grown in fairly rich, well-drained soil and make vines for arbors and fences. Gourds on climbing vines have more uniform shapes than those that develop resting on the ground.

October 23

October 24

October 25

Ablaze in autumn color, a blueberry field
proves irresistible to artists.

October 26

October 29

October 27

October 30

October 28

October 31

A bed of hay provides a comfortable place to carve pumpkins.

November

November 1
_____

November 2
_____

November 3
_____

November 4
_____

November 5
_____

November 6
_____

Seeds take flight from the pods of common milkweed (*Asclepias syriaca*).

November 7

November 10

November 8

November 11

November 9

November 12

An informal bittersweet wreath captures a carefree country style.

November 13

November 16

November 14

November 17

November 15

November 18

November 19

November 22

November 20

November 23

November 21

November 24

November 25

November 28

November 26

November 29

November 27

November 30

An old birch tree showers its golden foliage on freshly fallen snow.

December

December 1

December 4

December 2

December 5

December 3

December 6

Against a blue-painted door, scarlet winterberries herald the holiday season.

December 7

December 8

December 9

Decorated trees and a fresh blanket of
snow create a magical winter scene.

December 10

December 13

December 11

December 14

December 12

December 15

December 16

December 19

December 17

The Decorated Garden

Decorate your garden as you would your home. Hang homemade wreaths or swags from arbors or from old weathered doors. Place bouquets of winterberry atop urns and artifacts, or make grapevine balls, wrap them with fairy lights, and hang them in trees. And don't forget the birds: roll pine cones first in peanut butter and then in birdseed and hang from evergreens.

December 18

December 20

December 23

December 21

December 24

December 22

December 25

The poinsettia sport 'Hot Pink' was born and raised in Maine.

December 26
_____

December 29
_____

December 27
_____

December 30
_____

December 28
_____

December 31
_____

An ancient apple tree gives generously in every season: cool shade in summer; abundant fruit in fall; lacy beauty in winter, hinting at spring blossoms to come.

ISBN 0-89272-561-3
Printed in China
FCI
5 4 3 2 1

Down East Books / Camden, Maine
1-800-766-1670
www.downeastbooks.com

Award winning photographer Lynn Karlin has had her work published in *Country Living Gardener, Gardens Illustrated,* and Better Homes & Gardens publications, among others. Her specialty is gardens, and her favorite territory is her home ground of Maine.

Some of the images in this daybook come from the bestselling *Gardens Maine Style* (photos by Lynn Karlin, text by Rebecca Sawyer-Fay). Lynn's first book was *Maine Farm: A Year of Country Life (1991).*